D1549697

SO YOU THINK YOU KNOW?

LYMINGTON

Produced by The Francis Frith Collection
exclusively for

OTTAKAR'S

www.ottakars.co.uk

First published in the United Kingdom in 2005 by The Francis Frith Collection®

Hardback edition published in 2005 ISBN 1-84567-818-4

Text and Design copyright The Francis Frith Collection®
Photographs copyright The Francis Frith Collection® except where indicated.

British Library Cataloguing in Publication Data

So You Think You Know? Lymington
Text adapted from original material supplied by Jude James

The Francis Frith Collection
Frith's Barn, Teffont,
Salisbury, Wiltshire SP3 5QP
Tel: +44 (0) 1722 716 376
Email: info@francisfrith.co.uk
www.francisfrith.co.uk

Printed and bound in England

Front Cover: **LYMINGTON, HIGH STREET c1955** LI48022t

The colour-tinting is for illustrative purposes only, and is not intended to be historically accurate

Aerial photographs reproduced under licence from Simmons Aerofilms Limited.

Every attempt has been made to contact copyright holders of illustrative material.
We will be happy to give full acknowledgement in future editions for any items not credited.
Any information should be directed to The Francis Frith Collection.

CONTENTS

LYMINGTON, QUAY STREET c1955 L148041

LYMINGTON MISCELLANY

For Lymingtonians the New Forest must have seemed like a reservoir of fresh game on their doorstep. William Thorner was arraigned in 1486 for taking a young hind at Whitley. William Holcombe took a buck at Lady Hill, a doe at La Estyate, a fawn at Hurst, a doe at Butts Lawn and another from Lyndhurst Park. He was bound over to be of good behaviour 'under pain of £10'. John Bakere was pardoned in 1391 for several offences, all carried out on Thursdays, including taking the king's venison, an ox, and two cows belonging to the Earl of Kent.

> The income for the priests serving the church came from a levy, called the tithe, of one-tenth on all agricultural produce and in the case of Lymington, on the salt produced. This meant that for every ten sheaves of corn harvested one went to the church and was stored in a tithe barn.

Lymington traders maintained close commercial contacts with Southampton merchants, as the following list of debts illustrates. In 1554 we find William Sibill of Lymington owing Thomas Harrison, a girdle maker, the sum of 3s 7d. In 1573 John Pamplyn owed the wealthiest Southampton merchant, Richard Goddard, 48s 4d, and in addition William Hunte owed him 40s 2d. In the same year, William Elliot and Thomas Burad owed Reynold Howse 49s 9d and 47s 9d respectively.

There were harsh punishments for not attending church on Sundays, which was to be kept sacred. In Lymington those who travelled for business on the Lord's Day were fined £1. Boatmen, perhaps because the weather was unpredictable, were treated more leniently and were fined only 5s. As Sunday was the only rest day the working population had an opportunity to gather for leisure pursuits. Church absenteeism was often due to men playing games. Those baiting bulls or bears or engaging in plays or sports in Lymington were fined 3s 4d. Those who could not pay were locked in the stocks.

Inoculation against smallpox, first introduced into this country by Lady Mary Wortley Montagu in about 1720, was further refined by Benjamin Jesty and Edward Jenner, quite independently of each other, by using cowpox serum. This treatment became the first major application of preventative medicine and by the 1780s every parish in the kingdom was paying to have its poor inhabitants treated.

In 1790 the Rev William Gilpin of Boldre described what must be one of the earliest women's friendly societies, established in Lymington. Lymington 'being a little sea-port, and frequented by the seamen of small coasting vessels, and boatmen, their wives are often put to inconveniences … by the absence of their husbands'. Membership was available to those aged between 15 and 50 years and of each 'It was required that she should be a parishioner, of good character, and in good health at the time of her entrance'. Initially the prime aim was to provide for women during their lying-in.

There was no life-saving equipment on the first ferry commissioned by the Solent Sea Steam Packet Co. In 1840 the Lymington company was able to commission its own all-iron steam paddle ferry. It was built by a Southampton shipbuilder for £2,275 and delivered in May 1841. It had a 25-horsepower engine and a draught of only 3 feet 4 inches so it was suitable for the shallow waters of Lymington River at all tides. Although there was no life-saving equipment, it did have water closets for men by the paddle box and for the ladies in their own cabin.

Marconi carried out some of his earliest wireless experiments using Lymington ferries. In 1866 a fine iron-built paddler, the 'Mayflower', was added to the fleet, and in 1897 it was chartered by Guglielimo Marconi to develop his experiments in wireless communications over water. It was the first vessel in the world to be fitted with a receiving apparatus. The transmitter was sited on a hill behind Totland Bay, Isle of Wight, and from there the signals were broadcast to the vessel. The experiments proved successful and represented the first major step in the development of shore to ship communication.

LYMINGTON, HIGH STREET c1960 L148175

LYMINGTON, THE ROYAL YACHT CLUB c1955 LI48030

The great granite monument at Walhampton, designed by George Draper, is clearly visible when looking eastwards from the High Street. It commemorates the life and services of Sir Harry Burrard Neale (1765-1840) both to the nation, as a sailor, and to his native town of Lymington as a benefactor and politician. It was completed in 1841 at a cost of £1,482, the money being raised by public subscription. The monument was built by George Banks of Lymington from Cornish granite and remains an enduring landmark to the present day.

For folk who disliked physical exercise Lymington had the Lazy Club, founded in the late 18th century. Members were not to engage in activities such as working. Even when standing in the street, the member was expected to support himself against 'a House, a Post, or other convenient Thing'. Even those members engaged in the seafaring life had to be careful to 'not, on any Pretence row in the Heat of the Day. It will be far more honourable to lay down and sleep'. Membership was addressed 'TO THE FREE AND EASY and such as are desirous of attaining A GOOD OLD AGE!'.

The inventor of the hansom cab designed Lymington's Catholic church. The arrival of the Roman Catholic Joseph Weld at Pylewell in 1801 paved the way for Lymington Catholics to have their own church. He purchased properties in the High Street in 1857 and Joseph Aloysius Hansom (1803-82), an experienced architect of Catholic churches, was engaged to design the church. The consecration ceremony was conducted by Bishop Thomas Grant of Southwark on 18 May 1859. While preparing the site a workman, George Preston, died from the poisonous fumes released on opening old vaults. Several other workmen were overcome and became ill.

New Forest ponies once ranged freely around Lymington. However, the New Forest Act of 1964, amongst numerous provisions, required that the forest perambulation should be fenced with cattle grids across every road that crossed its boundary. As a consequence of this measure, Lymington lost what was both an attractive feature for visitors and tourists and a considerable nuisance to residents. Until the Act, the wandering commoners' ponies grazed not only along the roadside but also, when they could get access, in people's gardens.

LYMINGTON, QUAY HILL c1955 LI48048

Dentists used to visit Lymington from outside the town. From 1850 until about 1877 Mr Jones of Southampton came on the second Monday each month. After his son joined him, another visit was made on the fourth Monday. They advertised: 'Patients requiring the Nitrous Oxide Gas ensuring all immunity from Pain, will kindly make a written appointment a few days previously'. Another Southampton dentist, J McLachlan, held a surgery on the first and third Tuesdays each month. He offered 'A complete set of Teeth from Five Guineas, constructed upon the most approved principles'. Mr R W Reid became a resident dentist in the 1920s.

The novelist Dennis Wheatley bought Grove House in Church Lane in 1944 for £6,400 and wrote 30 of his popular novels whilst living there. For relaxation Wheatley, like Winston Churchill, enjoyed bricklaying. He has left one visible piece of his work in the form of a serpentine (or crinkle-crankle) wall in Church Lane. He sold the property in 1968 for £29,000 and the house was demolished the following year. The site was then developed as a neo-Georgian residential estate.

The Domesday record of Lymington (named Lentune) shows the tiny community occupied in agricultural activities. Place-name scholars suggest that 'Lentune' had been abridged and the middle syllable omitted. About forty years later the town is named both Lemynton and Limenton. Scholars took Lemen to be a Celtic word, meaning elm tree, given to the river. Later the Anglo-Saxon word for a settlement, 'tun', was added, Lemen-tun. Another explanation for the name is that Lemen is derived from a much older Latin word, Lemana, meaning marsh. This argues that the name actually means Marsh-tun, a farm or settlement by the marsh.

An annual three-day fair was held in Lymington, 'on the eve, on the day and on the morrow of St Matthew the Apostle', 20-22 September. John Boucher of Harfleur attacked a ship plying from the Isle of Wight to Lymington. It was carrying merchandise valued at £2,000, specifically earmarked for the fair of 1411. On board there was £254 'of gold and silver of the king's coin', eight 'pakkes' of woollen cloth valued at £300, ten 'pakkes' of linen cloth 'to the value of £400', other packs and bales of mercery, and a cargo of jewels worth £500.

LYMINGTON, HIGH STREET c1960 L148174

LYMINGTON, THE RIVER c1960 L148131

The office of mayor is first recorded for Lymington in 1412 when Stephen Holcombe is so described, and continued until abolished by local government reorganisation in 1974.

Throughout the 18th century Lymington's main industry was the manufacture of salt. Celia Fiennes visited Lymington in 1698 and noted that its 'greatest trade is by their Salterns'. She described how sea water flowed into ponds and was allowed to evaporate until a briny liquor remained. This was pumped into iron or copper pans situated in barn-like buildings where it was boiled dry, leaving a deposit of salt which was scraped off and collected in baskets. Around 1800 Lymington was producing approximately 5,200 tons of salt a year but by 1825 only three salterns were operating.

King John gave Southampton jurisdiction over several harbours, including Lymington. Southampton's mayor acted as admiral, operating through admiralty courts. Around 1324 Geoffrey Scurlag, William Culhout and 18 other Lymington men were arraigned for two offences. The first claimed they had maltreated Walter Depedene, a court official; the second that they had taken for their own use customs on salt, corn, barley and oats, valued at 11s, landed by the 'Le Johette' and furthermore customs valued at £5 on cloth, wax and other merchandise landed from the 'Port Joy'. The jury found in favour of Southampton. Lymington had to pay £200 damages.

During the second phase of the Hundred Years War, the south coast was subjected to many raids by the French, the most dastardly being against the harbours of Yarmouth, Newtown and Newport on the Isle of Wight in the summer of 1377. Despite the persistence of a local tradition that Lymington was sacked and burned, there is no historical evidence of Lymington being raided .

So you think you know?
LYMINGTON

In the Middle Ages Lymington was an important commercial harbour. A mid 14th-century record shows the export of 4,000 quarters of salt and 600 sacks of wool, and the import of 1,800 tuns of wine and 3,700 fish. A boat belonging to John Haylys left Southampton for Lymington on 16 November 1509 with four quarters of bay salt. A cargo of 1,000 hake arrived in Southampton on 3 February 1510 en route for Lymington. On 25 February 1510 John Rogers of Lymington sailed carrying two tuns of ale and William Mayn's boat took 200 flat fish to Lymington.

Isabella de Fortibus, the lady of the manor of Lymington, was obliged to go to court in 1280 to try to establish that her hunting dogs, used in the New Forest, and those of 'her men at Liminton' should not be expeditated, that is, subject to the cutting back of their claws. It was agreed that Isabella and 'her men of Old and New Lymington' could avoid this stricture provided they proved it was an established custom.

LYMINGTON, OLD LYMINGTON c1965 L148212

A surviving fragment of a medieval house is preserved in a stone wall of the Red House, next to the post office. This together with parts of the church and some foundation walling in Church Lane is all that remains visible of Lymington's ancient past.

The first known reference to a church at Lymington is in the second charter of Christchurch Priory. Dated about 1155, it records, 'The church at Bolra with its chapels of Limnetona and Brokenhurst'. Lymington church had the status of a chapel served originally by priests from Christchurch Priory. The Lymington parishioners were obliged to 'visit their mother church at Bolra with a fit offering on St John Baptist's day' in return for having their own cemetery at Lymington church. The church was dedicated to St Thomas the Apostle.

13

It was important for the conduct of good government that the burgesses of Lymington should attend meetings regularly and participate in running the town's business. Severe penalties were enjoined against those who failed to do so. Even as early as 1584 it had been ordered that any burgess failing to attend a meeting called by the mayor, unless he had a good excuse, would be fined either 5s or suffer 'two daies and two nyghtes imprysonement'.

LYMINGTON, THE HARBOUR SIDE c1965 L148213

LYMINGTON, HIGH STREET c1955   L148049

In the first town book we find that Lymington has weavers, tailors, drapers, innkeepers and tipplers; the innkeepers providing then, as now, the ever-important sustenance and accommodation for townsfolk and visitors alike. The export and processing of wool into cloth was of central importance to both the national and local economy. The town sustained cloth workers as the occupation of weaver indicates. Wool was an important export from Lymington throughout the late 16th and the first half of the 17th century; in 1615 eighteen loads are exported, 16 loads in 1616, 21 loads in 1617 and so on.

The Market Cross had to be maintained at the expense of the borough. Being in many ways the centrepiece of urban trade it was essential that the market street around it should be kept in good condition. It is easy to visualize how the passage of animals to and from the market, and the mud carried on the wheels of carts, would soon turn the street into a quagmire so it comes as no surprise to find in 1640 the burgesses spending 10s on ten tons of pebble stones to be set about the market cross.

The expenses of maintaining the implements of punishment, which were sited close to the Market House, were met by the Lymington burgesses. The various punishments included the stocks, ducking stool, pillory, whipping post and the blind house or lock-up.

The majority of the burgesses of Lymington and doubtless many of the townsfolk supported the Parliamentary cause against the king when the Civil War broke out in 1642. Such support was sustained by the strong nonconformist element amongst the burgesses. However, when Charles I was imprisoned in Carisbrooke Castle, the mayor, Bernard Knapton, supported the Royalist cause. Apparently only one major skirmish took place at or near Lymington when three troops of Royalist horse were attacked by a Parliamentary force, killing 300.

In 1662 the government introduced a Hearth Tax, which required the sum of 2s to be levied on each hearth or stove in every house whose rental value was above £1 per annum. In 1665 New Lymington had 95 households of which 30 had one hearth, 27 had two, and 6 had seven or eight hearths. Old Lymington had 53 households, 23 had one hearth, 16 had two, while one house, Buckland Manor, had 19. Because of poverty, 27 in the borough and 23 in Old Lymington were excused payment.

Some of the belongings of shoemaker Edward Smith, mentioned in his will dated 1676, include his main bed, with a tester, a feather mattress, a bolster, a pair of pillows, sheets and blankets (valued at £5) and a warming pan. Kept in chests were wearing apparel, bedding, tablecloths and napkins. He had five candlesticks. In the kitchen were two brass kettles, two skillets, a frying pan, an iron pot, tongs and hangers in the hearth, an iron dripping pan, a grater, a salt cellar and a pepper box. Edward was evidently literate for he owned five books.

Politics were central in the life of the Lymington burgesses during the Georgian period. Lymington was a 'pocket' borough, whose small electorate was dominated by the established Burrard family, allied with the Powletts (Dukes of Bolton). In the 29 parliaments called between 1754 and 1831 there were no contested elections for the two Lymington MPs. In the last contested election of 1710 the two successful candidates had between them only 64 votes out of an electorate of 78. At one time Edward Gibbon, the author of 'The Decline and Fall of the Roman Empire', represented Lymington.

LYMINGTON, HIGH STREET c1955   L148051

LYMINGTON, ST THOMAS'S CHURCH c1955 L148011

Lymington built its first workhouse for the poor in 1738 at a cost of £248 10s. It was to provide basic but decent accommodation within an environment of compulsory employment. Only the poorest were accommodated. A master was appointed to oversee the general management at an annual salary of £10. Sick and infirm inmates were given medical attention by local doctors but the workhouse also had its own resident dispenser in the person of Henry Hackman. The Old Poor Law system, after more than 230 years, was overtaken by new legislation in 1834. Lymington became the centre of a Poor Law Union comprising the surrounding parishes of Boldre, Brockenhurst, Milford, Milton and Hordle. A new large workhouse (the 'Union') was built near the old parish workhouse on the top of the hill facing New Lane; this building still survives.

In the 18th century a number of epidemic diseases were prevalent and probably the worst of these was smallpox. In 1741 Lymington's overseers and churchwardens purchased a house known as the 'Doggs Kennell' which was to be refurbished so that it could be used to house those with smallpox or other infectious diseases. It became known as the 'Pest House'.

Illegitimacy was one of the social problems confronting the overseers of the poor and churchwardens. If the father's name could be found by examining the pregnant woman under oath he might be persuaded to marry the girl, or if he could not, to contribute to the child's maintenance. In 1780 a Lymington man, James Alexander, was ordered that if he did not contribute towards the maintenance of his son, also James, 'the parish will endeavour to get him on board a Man-of-War'. In fact James must have gone into the Newfoundland trade, for his marriage is recorded at St John's, Newfoundland in 1836, where he is described as 'of Lymington'.

LYMINGTON, THE FERRY c1955 LI48014

Lymington was linked to the turnpike road system from 1765 with a road running northward from the town through the New Forest to Southampton. The mid to late 18th century saw considerable improvements in road construction which was particularly encouraged under the turnpike system, and also marked advances in vehicle design. By the 1780s Lymington had a coach, the Diligence, making return journeys from Southampton on Tuesdays, Thursdays and Saturdays. Commercial wagons travelled to Ringwood on Mondays and Saturdays and to and from Christchurch on Saturdays.

In Georgian times smuggling was an important part of Lymington's economic life. In the 1670s, Thomas Baskerville noted that Lymington was a convenient spot for 'stealing wines ashore, and that perhaps of late has contributed to their wealth, for here are now built some handsome houses.' Lymington, lying in the centre of an area of coastal marsh and creeks, became an ideal centre for smuggling. A number of affrays occurred between the forces of law, order and the smugglers. In July 1799 the customs officer, Charles Colborne, was shot dead during one of these engagements.

Coals from Newcastle and Sunderland were brought in to Lymington by sea for both the salt industry and for domestic use. Coal was an important commodity, and Lymington Corporation employed men known as 'coal meters' who measured the cargo into baskets.

One of the old-established businesses in Lymington was that of the musical instrument retailer, Klitz. A firm established in 1789 by a refugee from war-torn Europe named Glitz (the name was later changed to Klitz). On an occasion in July 1827 Colonel Peter Hawker, himself an accomplished musician, visited Klitz and expressed his high opinion of 'old Klitz the Clementi of the place'. The business flourished for many decades until commercial pressures obliged it to close in 1981. Today a blue plaque is affixed to the front of Klitz's former shop to commemorate this early retailing establishment.

LYMINGTON, TITHE BARN ZZZ03658 (Author's Collection)

23

Lymington's first school was founded by George Fulford of Toller Fratrum in Dorset, elected burgess in 1667. It was a grammar school for boys, who were to be 'taught and trained up in learning and the true Protestant religion, and more especially the knowledge of Latin, Greek, writing, arithmetic and good life'. The schoolmaster's income came from an endowment but he had to pay himself to repair any broken windows. The exact location of this first school is not known but only 20 years after its foundation the school moved into the upper room of the town hall.

In 1832 it was decided to provide gas lighting in the borough. To start the project, £3,000 was raised, while two local doctors proposed forming the Lymington Gas and Coke Company to manufacture and supply the gas. Iron columns for the lights were presented by Sir Harry Burrard Neale while his brother, George Burrard, supplied the lamps. A large ornate commemorative cast-iron gas standard was installed opposite the town hall, which was later transferred to a position outside the parish church. After the Second World War it was removed to a location near the Royal Lymington Yacht Clubhouse (see page 30).

LYMINGTON, THE FERRY c1955 L148019

So you think you know?
LYMINGTON

In December 1851 the Lymington council received a letter from the Board of Health stating that the prevalence of fever and diarrhoea at Lymington gave strong grounds for supposing that the population was suffering from a neglect of sanitary precautions. A later report of 1867 described Broad Lane as 'filthy and unwholesome', Station Street as 'becoming offensive from the want of sewerage' and 'the state of the Quays where the principal sewers of the Town now empty themselves' as disgusting. Even the Lymington Chronicle had reported that the streets 'in some places have the appearance of an open bog'.

The Southampton and Dorchester Railway opened in 1847 and Brockenhurst, lying four miles to the north, became the nearest station to Lymington. In August 1853 a public meeting pressed for a branch line from Brockenhurst to Lymington, which was completed in 1858. The new town station was opened in September 1859. The line continued to a jetty, opened in July 1861, for Isle of Wight ferries. Later, a 70-yard long viaduct, supported on steel piles, was constructed to carry the line over the Lymington River to a new terminus, named Lymington Pier, opened on 1 May 1884.

LYMINGTON, THE ISLE OF WIGHT FERRY c1955 L148052

As Lymington's salt-making industry declined, two influential figures ushered in the important yacht-building industry. The first was Joseph Weld of Pylewell. The second was Thomas Inman, a boat builder who on a visit to the Solent saw the potential of Lymington as a yacht-building centre. Inman established himself on the Lymington River in 1820. His first boat, the 20-ton 'Hind', was completed the same year. The 85-ton cutter, 'Arrow', was constructed for Joseph Weld in 1821. The largest yacht built by the Inman boat yard was the 366-ton 'Fortuna' in 1876.

In the 19th century there were 17 inns and public houses in the borough of Lymington of which three made provision for posting and travellers, namely, the Angel, the Anchor and Hope and the Nag's Head. Of the others no fewer than six were clustered around the quay area. Beer and ale were brewed locally and there were five breweries operating.

The vogue for sea-bathing began in the mid 18th century, and Lymington's first bath house was built in 1777. However, a guide to watering places published in 1806 says: 'considered solely as a watering place, Lymington has little that can recommend it.' Perhaps it was observations like this that led to the foundation of the Lymington Bath Improvement Company in 1833. Close on £6,000 was raised for a venture committed to erecting more commodious baths and improving access to them. The charming main building (which survives today as the headquarters of the Town Sailing Club) was designed by William Bartlett.

Lymington townsfolk celebrated the victorious outcome of the Crimean War in 1856. The corporation felt a durable symbol should be provided and in 1858 the mayor of Lymington made a request for one of the Russian guns captured in the Crimea to be given to the town. The request was granted and an iron carriage, made at Woolwich Arsenal, and paid for by public subscription, supported the gun, which was displayed at the north end of New Street. In due course an even greater conflict was to see its removal in 1941 as scrap to aid the war effort.

The foundation stone for Lymington's new town hall was laid on 12 February 1913. The building served the enlarged borough for fifty years, by which time it became too small to meet the new demands of local government. So in April 1962 the borough council confirmed a decision to build another town hall on a site in Avenue Road. Despite some cries of 'ugly building' and 'more like a barracks than a Town Hall', work progressed so that by the summer of 1966 the building was ready for its official opening by the Queen.

Lymington people did their bit for the war effort during the First World War. Home Mead, the site of the present post office, was requisitioned and turned into a convalescent home for wounded New Zealand soldiers. Girls at the junior school collected money to purchase socks for them. In 1916 schoolboys in the town collected six hundredweight of horse chestnuts which were used to make charcoal for gasmask filters. Sphagnum moss was also gathered from the nearby forest heathland which, after sterilising, formed a useful absorbent in wound dressings.

The first motorcar in Lymington was said to belong to Dr Pithie. Its registration number was AA 4.

LYMINGTON, AN AERIAL VIEW OF THE LAUNDRY
c1930 ZZZ03681
(Author's Collection)

LYMINGTON, A 1932 GAS COLUMN ZZZ03673 (Author's Collection)

LYMINGTON QUIZ QUESTIONS

1. What name was given to Lymington in Domesday book?

2. Who granted the first charter to Lymington?

3. Salt manufacture was a major industry in Lymington. What was the source for the salt?

4. On which day of the week is the market held in Lymington?

5. There were different overlords of Lymington at different times. Which family held the overlordship in the 13th century?

6. How many ships did Lymington supply for the King's navy in 1345?

7. To which saint is Lymington parish church dedicated?

8. In which monarch's reign did Lymington first return two members to Parliament?

9. The author of 'The Decline and Fall of the Roman Empire' was for a time one of Lymington's MPs. What was his name?

10. Which Lymington nonconformist church was first established in the late 17th century?

LYMINGTON, HIGH STREET c1955 L148091

LYMINGTON c1965 L148218

11. Who was the principal figure who financed Lymington's first Grammar School?

12. ...and where did he come from?

13. Which prominent Lymington family supported the rebellion of the Duke of Monmouth in 1685?

14. Until the mid 18th century Lymington port and harbour was under the jurisdiction of another town.
Which town was that?

15. When was the bridge built across the Lymington River?

LYMINGTON, THE HIGH STREET FROM THE CHURCH 1958 L148142

16. What was the name of the family that dominated Lymington politics for more than two centuries?

17. ...and where was its main residence?

18. Several contingents of French troops were based at Lymington at the time of the Napoleonic Wars.
In 1795 they were despatched to invade which part of Brittany?

19. Joseph Weld of Pylewell had a great enthusiasm for yachting and was largely responsible for founding the first dedicated yacht building firm. Under what name did it operate?

20. Who was the main proposer of the suspension bridge designed to link Lymington to Walhampton in 1832?

LYMINGTON, QUAY HILL c1960   L148088

LYMINGTON, THE RIVER c1960   L148131

21. In which year was a system of street gas lighting installed in Lymington?

22. There is a large granite obelisk at Walhampton, clearly visible from Lymington's High Street. Who does it commemorate?

23. Lymington's town hall stood in the centre of the High Street for many decades. When was it demolished?

24. What kind of business did the Klitz family run in Lymington from 1789-1981?

25. What connection has Joseph A Hansom, the inventor of the hansom cab, with Lymington?

26. Lymington had its first branch railway in 1858.
From which station did the branch run?

27. Lymington did not have a proper water supply until 1880.
Where was the well that provided this supply situated?

LYMINGTON, QUAY HILL c1955 L148021

LYMINGTON, THE FERRY c1955 LI48024

28. For what purpose was the Lymington-Isle of Wight paddle
steamer 'Mayflower' hired by Marconi?

29. In what part of Lymington was the town's second Anglican
church built?

30. Home Mead, once a substantial house, was used for what purpose during the First World War?

31. To which monarch was Lymington Cottage Hospital dedicated?

LYMINGTON, THE QUAY c1955 L148086

LYMINGTON, HIGH STREET c1955 L148068

32. The Wellworthy piston and piston ring factories were major employers in Lymington. Who founded the firm?

33. Lymington had one of the country's earliest community centres. In what year was it opened?

34. What famous and popular novelist lived in Lymington after the Second World War?

35. In what year was Lymington's first workhouse constructed?

36. As a result of the Poor Law Amendment Act of 1834 Lymington became the centre of a union of parishes which included, Boldre, Brockenhurst and Milton. But there were two others: can you name them?

37. What Parliamentary Act abolished the old system of appointed burgesses in Lymington, and replaced it by one in which councillors were elected?

38. What was the name of the first ferry steamer on the Lymington to Isle of Wight service introduced in 1830?

39. In what year was Lymington's first commercial bank established?

40. What was the name of the largest yacht (366 tons) built at the Inman boatyard?

41. What durable legacy of the Crimean War was displayed in Lymington until 1941?

LYMINGTON, THE ROYAL YACHT CLUB c1955 LI48030

42. The National School in Lymington, founded in 1836 and closed in 1991, is now used to house what?

43. Only one stray bomb dropped on Lymington town during the Second World War. Which business premises did it destroy?

44. Lymington's first purpose-built theatre was constructed in New Lane in 1771. Who was the first manager?

45. In what year was Lymington's football club founded?

LYMINGTON, THE SWIMMING POOL c1955 L148072

46. In July 1799 Charles Colborne of Lymington was killed whilst exercising his official duty as what?

LYMINGTON, HIGH STREET c1955 L148117

LYMINGTON, HIGH STREET c1955   L148049

47. What purpose did the pound in New Lane serve?

48. Which side did Lymington support at the outbreak of the Civil War in 1642?

LYMINGTON, ST THOMAS'S CHURCH c1955 L148118

49. Lymington corporation had taken responsibility for running the fire service in 1889, but how many years were to elapse before they purchased a motorised engine?

50. In what year did work start on the new, long-awaited Lymington Hospital?

LYMINGTON, HIGH STREET c1960 LI48188

LYMINGTON, HIGH STREET c1960 L148175

LYMINGTON QUIZ ANSWERS

1. Lentune.

2. William de Redvers.

3. The sea.

4. Saturday.

5. The de Redvers.

6. Nine.

7. St Thomas the Apostle (not St Thomas à Beckett).

8. Queen Elizabeth I.

9. Edward Gibbon.

10. The Baptist Church.

11. George Fulford.

12. Toller Fratrum, Dorset.

13. The Dore family.

14. Southampton.

15. 1731.

16. Burrard.

17. Walhampton House.

18. Quiberon.

19. Inman (Thomas Inman, later G & J Inman).

20. R A Grove.

21. 1832.

22. Sir Harry Burrard Neale, the local benefactor and politician.

23. 1858.

24. Suppliers of musical instruments and, later, audio equipment.

25. He was the architect of the Roman Catholic Church.

26. Brockenhurst.

27. At Ampress (or Ampress Farm).

LYMINGTON QUIZ ANSWERS

28. For experiments in wireless communication.

29. Woodside.

30. A convalescent home for wounded soldiers.

31. Edward VII.

32. John Howlett.

33. 1946.

34. Denis Wheatley.

35. 1738.

36. Hordle and Milford.

37. The Municipal Corporation Act of 1835.

38. The paddle steamer 'Glasgow'.

39. 1788.

40. The 'Fortuna'.

41. A Russian cannon.

42. The St Barbe Museum and Art Gallery.

43. Ford's furniture shop.

44. William Shatford.

45. 1876.

46. A customs officer.

47. To hold animals that strayed in the town.

48. The Parliamentarians.

49. 39 years (1889-1928).

50. 2004.

GOUDHURST, MEASURING THE HOPS 1904 52571

GENERAL HISTORY QUIZ QUESTIONS

1. Which 20th-century Prime Minister was a proficient bricklayer and a member of the union?

2. In Victorian times, what powerful substance did many fashionable society ladies use to spice up their afternoon tea parties?

3. What was the first battle of the English Civil War on 23 October 1642?

4. Who was Queen Victoria's first Prime Minister?

5. Which Michigan-born dentist was arrested in Canada for the murder of his wife in London?

6. For what crime was Titus Oates pilloried in the stocks and flogged every year?

7. What crime was committed by Burke and Hare?

8. What language was Elizabeth I not fluent in? German, French, Latin, or Italian?

9. In 1834 six Dorset farm labourers were transported to Australia. By what name are these men usually known?

HORNING, ON THE BROADS 1902 48108

10. At which battle was Richard III slain?

11. Who was the first Prime Minister to live at Chequers?

12. Who was the leader of the Women's Social and Political Union?

13. What year were women granted the vote on the Isle of Man?
    1881, 1902, 1912, or 1946?

RHYL, DONKEYS ON THE SANDS 1891 29151

14. Which king signed the Magna Carta in 1215 at Runnymede?

15. In which city was the infamous Peterloo Massacre on 16 August 1819?

16. Who were the mother and father of Elizabeth I?

17. Before the French Revolution in 1789, who is reported to have said 'Let them eat cake'?

18. Who wore two shirts in which to be executed, and why?

NEWQUAY, THE HARBOUR 1894 33522

19. Which queen was known as Bloody Mary?

20. Who was the only English pope?

21. Which British king married May of Teck?

22. At the outbreak of World War I, who was the British Prime Minister?

23. What great structure, designed by Joseph Paxton, was built in 1851?

24. What were the names of the two princes believed to have been murdered in the Tower of London in 1483?

25. What unusual accident eventually caused the death of the Prince of Wales, eldest son of George II?

26. Which of Dickens's novels depicts the struggles and strife of factory workers in Victorian England?

EVERSLEY, THE WHITE HART 1906 57011

27. How old was William Shakespeare when he got married? 24, 25, 19, or 18?

28. What crime occurred on 8 August 1963 that shocked public opinion in Britain?

29. Who had to hide in an oak tree to save his life after a military defeat?

30. After Henry VIII's Dissolution of the Monasteries, what are some of the new owners of the monastery buildings rumoured to have done with some of the illuminated manuscripts they found?

KING'S LYNN, HIGH STREET 1908 60023

BOURNEMOUTH, INVALID'S WALK 1900 45226

31. In July 1888, 1,500 female employees went on strike at a factory at Bow in East London. What did they manufacture?

32. Who was the Irish saint who legend says saw the Loch Ness Monster in Scotland?
St Columba, St Patrick, St Andrew, or St Aidan?

33. Which English woman made this prophecy:
'Carriages without horses shall go, And accidents fill the world with woe. Around the world thoughts shall fly, In the twinkling of an eye.'?

34. Which tax was levied between 1696 and 1851?

35. How long did the Hundred Years' War last? 116 years, 94 years, 100 years, or 108 years?

36. Who was called the 'Old Pretender'?

37. In 1629 William Harvey published the details of a discovery he had made. What was it?

38. Put these wars and battles in the order in which they took place:
   A. The Battle of Agincourt
   B. The Battle of Hastings
   C. Marston Moor
   D. Wars of the Roses

39. In British army slang, what was a 'dead man'?

40. When was the Poll Tax first introduced in England?

SAFFRON WALDEN, FRY'S GARDEN 1907 58821

CLOVELLY, POST OFFICE, TRANSFER OF MAIL 1936 87551

41. Who was the first Prime Minister of Britain?

42. What is pannage?

78

43. What were the Welshmen of the Rebecca Riots, who dressed up as women, protesting against?

44. How many people did the 1715 Riot Act have to be read to, in order for them to be guilty of a felony, and liable to the punishment of death? 6, 12, 27, or 250?

CHALFORD, THE VILLAGE 1910 62713

45. What was the joint stock company, the South Sea Company, set up in 1711 to trade in?

46. In the Middle Ages, a split stick was used by royal officials to record sums of money paid. Notches were cut on it representing payments. What was it called?

EASTBOURNE, THE PIER 1925 77946

47. When did the Union Jack achieve its present pattern?

48. In 1752, September 2 was followed by September 14. What was the name of the new calendar system that involved this adjustment?

NEWBY BRIDGE, THE SWAN HOTEL 1914 67414

49. Coffee houses were patronised by literary giants such as Dryden, Johnson, and Pope. How many coffee houses were there in London in the 18th century?
10, 50, 250, or 1800?

50. Who was the first British Prime Minister to live at 10 Downing Street?

TENBY 1890 28091

GENERAL HISTORY QUIZ ANSWERS

1. Winston Churchill.

2. Opium.

3. Edgehill.

4. Lord Melbourne.

5. Dr Crippen. He buried her body in the basement of his London house.

6. For giving false evidence against Catholics.

7. They murdered people and sold their corpses to unscrupulous surgeons for dissection.

8. German.

9. The Tolpuddle Martyrs.

10. The Battle of Bosworth Field.

11. Lloyd George.

12. Emmeline Pankhurst.

13. 1881.

14. King John.

15. Manchester.

16. Henry VIII and Anne Boleyn.

17. Marie Antoinette.

18. Charles I. The weather was cold and he did not want to be seen shivering.

19. Mary I, the daughter of Henry VIII and Catherine of Aragon. She married Philip II of Spain, and was a devout Catholic. She earned her nickname from her persecution of Protestants.

20. Adrian IV, born Nicholas Brakespeare in 1100.

21. George V (she was known in this country as Mary).

22. Herbert Asquith.

23. The Crystal Palace.

24. Edward V and his brother Richard Duke of York, the sons of Edward IV.

25. He was hit on the head by a cricket ball.

GENERAL HISTORY QUIZ ANSWERS

26. 'Hard Times', published in 1854.

27. 18.

28. The Great Train Robbery.

29. Charles II.

30. They used them as lavatory paper.

31. Matches. They worked at the Bryant and May factory.

32. St Columba, born cAD521.

33. Mother Shipton, born in Norfolk in 1485.

34. Window Tax, which was payable on a house with more than six windows.

35. 116 years, between 1337 and 1453.

36. James III (the son of James II). In 1715 he gathered together a force of 10,000 men and invaded England. The Jacobites fought their way as far as Preston, where they were dispersed.

37. The circulation of the blood. He was physician extraordinary to James I.

38. B (1066) A (1415) D (1455-85) C (1644).

39. An empty bottle.

40. In 1222, on every person over the age of 14.

41. Robert Walpole. As first Lord of the Treasury between 1721 and 1742 he presided over the cabinet.

42. The right of tenants to graze their swine in the woods of a manor.

43. They destroyed turnpike houses, being unhappy about the levels of tolls.

44. 12.

45. Slaves in Latin America.

46. A tally.

47. In 1801, when the cross of St Patrick was added to the crosses of St George and St Andrew.

48. The Gregorian Calendar.

49. 1800.

50. Sir Robert Walpole (1676-1745).

Ottakar's Bookshops

Ottakar's bookshops, the first of which opened in Brighton in 1988, can now be found in over 130 towns and cities across the United Kingdom. Expansion was gradual throughout the 1990s, but the chain has expanded rapidly in recent years, with many new shop openings and the acquisition of shops from James Thin and Hammicks.

Ottakar's has always known that a shop's local profile is as important, if not more important, than the chain's national profile, and has encouraged its staff to make their shops a part of the local community, tailoring stock to suit the area and forging links with local schools and businesses.

Local history has always been a strong area for Ottakar's, and the company has published its own award winning local history titles, based on text written by its customers, in recent years.

With a reputation for friendly, intelligent and enthusiastic booksellers, warm, inviting shops with an excellent range of books and related products, Ottakar's is now one of the UK's most popular booksellers. In 2003 and then again in 2004 it won the prestigious Best Bookselling Company of the Year Award at the British Book Awards.

Ottakar's has commissioned The Francis Frith Collection to create a series of town history books similar to this volume, as well as a range of stylish gift products, all illustrated with historical photographs.

Participating Ottakar's bookshops can be found in the following towns and cities:

Aberdeen	Fareham	Ormskirk
Abergavenny	Farnham	Petersfield
Aberystwyth	Folkestone	Portsmouth
Andover	Glasgow	Poole
Ashford	Gloucester	Redhill
Ayr	Greenwich	St Albans
Banbury	Grimsby	St Andrews
Barnstaple	Guildford	St Neots
Basildon	Harrogate	St Helier
Berkhamsted	Hastings	Salisbury
Bishop's Stortford	Haywards Heath	Sheffield
Boston	Hemel Hempstead	Stafford
Brentwood	High Wycombe	Staines
Bromley	Horsham	Stevenage
Bury St Edmunds	Huddersfield	Sutton Coldfield
Camberley	Inverness	Teddington
Canterbury	Isle of Wight	Tenterden
Carmarthen	Kendal	Tiverton
Chatham	King's Lynn	Torquay
Chelmsford	Kirkcaldy	Trowbridge
Cheltenham	Lancaster	Truro
Cirencester	Lincoln	Tunbridge Wells
Coventry	Llandudno	Twickenham
Crawley	Loughborough	Walsall
Darlington	Lowestoft	Wilmslow and
Dorchester	Luton	Alderley Edge
Douglas, Isle of Man	Lymington	Wells
Dumfries	Maidenhead	Weston-super-Mare
Dundee	Maidstone	Windsor
East Grinstead	Market Harborough	Witney
Eastbourne	Milton Keynes	Woking
Elgin	Newport	Worcester
Enfield	Newton Abbot	Yeovil
Epsom	Norwich	
Falkirk	Oban	

Francis Frith
Pioneer Victorian Photographer

Francis Frith, founder of the world-famous photographic archive, was a complex and multi-talented man. A devout Quaker and a highly successful Victorian businessman, he was philosophical by nature and pioneering in outlook. By 1855 he had already established a wholesale grocery business in Liverpool, and sold it for the astonishing sum of £200,000, which is the equivalent today of over £15,000,000. Now in his thirties, and captivated by the new science of photography, Frith set out on a series of pioneering journeys up the Nile and to the Near East.

INTRIGUE AND EXPLORATION

He was the first photographer to venture beyond the sixth cataract of the Nile. Africa was still the mysterious 'Dark Continent', and Stanley and Livingstone's historic meeting was a decade into the future. The conditions for picture taking confound belief. He laboured for hours in his wicker dark-room in the sweltering heat of the desert, while the volatile chemicals fizzed dangerously in their trays. Back in London he exhibited his photographs and was 'rapturously cheered' by members of the Royal Society. His reputation as a photographer was made overnight.

VENTURE OF A LIFE-TIME

By the 1870s the railways had threaded their way across the country, and Bank Holidays and half-day Saturdays had been made obligatory by Act of Parliament. All of a sudden the working man and his family were able to enjoy days out, take holidays, and see a little more of the world.

With typical business acumen, Francis Frith foresaw that these new tourists would enjoy having souvenirs to commemorate their days out. For the next thirty years he travelled the country by train and by pony and trap, producing fine photographs of seaside resorts and beauty spots that were keenly bought by millions of Victorians. These prints were painstakingly pasted into family albums and pored over during the dark nights of winter, rekindling precious memories of summer excursions. Frith's studio was soon supplying retail shops all over the country, and by 1890 F Frith & Co had become the greatest specialist photographic publishing company in the world, with over 2,000 sales outlets, and pioneered the picture postcard.

FRANCIS FRITH'S LEGACY

Francis Frith had died in 1898 at his villa in Cannes, his great project still growing. By 1970 the archive he created contained over a third of a million pictures showing 7,000 British towns and villages.

Frith's legacy to us today is of immense significance and value, for the magnificent archive of evocative photographs he created provides a unique record of change in the cities, towns and villages throughout Britain over a century and more. Frith and his fellow studio photographers revisited locations many times down the years to update their views, compiling for us an enthralling and colourful pageant of British life and character.

We are fortunate that Frith was dedicated to recording the minutiae of everyday life. For it is this sheer wealth of visual data, the painstaking chronicle of changes in dress, transport, street layouts, buildings, housing and landscape that captivates us so much today, offering us a powerful link with the past and with the lives of our ancestors.

Computers have now made it possible for Frith's many thousands of images to be accessed almost instantly. The archive offers every one of us an opportunity to examine the places where we and our families have lived and worked down the years. Its images, depicting our shared past, are now bringing pleasure and enlightenment to millions around the world a century and more after his death.

For further information visit: www.francisfrith.co.uk